·LEICESTERSHIRE·
RAILWAY MEMORIES

Leicestershire's county emblem has long been the fox. For those
engines allocated to the Mountsorrel stone workings, there was
a 'sub-shedding' at Leicester depot and the application of a
cabside fox symbol. Thus adorned, 56061 is seen at Leicester, in
the brilliant sunshine of 16 August 1987.

·LEICESTERSHIRE·
RAILWAY MEMORIES

JOHN STRETTON

Unicorn Books

For Judith, Adam and Tammy
They also serve who only sit and wait!

Other titles by the same author
Steam on Shed, Blandford Press
30 Years of Train Spotting, Unicorn Books

Other titles in the Unicorn Railway series
Midland through the Peak by Brian Radford
Great Central Rail Tour by John M. C. Healy
Cotswold Memories by Dennis Edwards and Ron Pigram

First published in 1989 by
UNICORN BOOKS,
16 Laxton Gardens,
Paddock Wood,
Kent TN12 6BB

© M. John Stretton 1989

British Library Cataloguing in Publication Data
Stretton, John
    Leicestershire railway memories
    1. Leicestershire. Railway services, history
    I. Title
    385′.09425′4

    ISBN 1-85241-007-8

Typeset by Vitaset, Paddock Wood.
Printed by Biddles Ltd
Guildford and King's Lynn.

Jacket illustration
The poplars of Birstall Golf Course have long been a local
landmark. An extremely rare sight, MR 'Coronation' 46251 *City
of Nottingham* travels the GC, at the head of RCTS *The East
Midlander Special*, bound for Swindon, 9 May 1964.

Contents

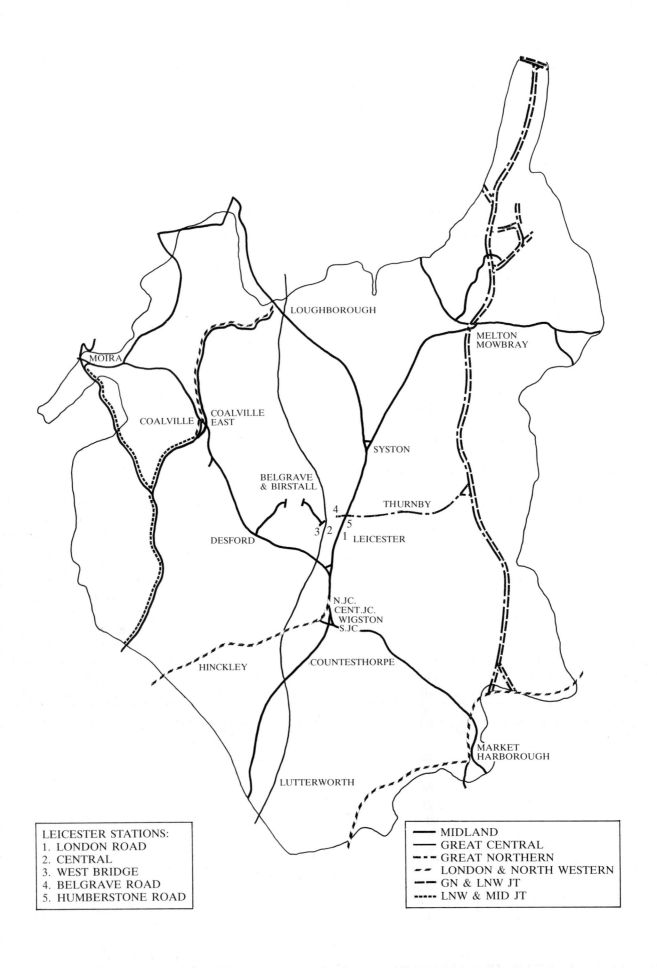

LOUGHBOROUGH

MELTON
MOWBRAY

MOIRA

COALVILLE

COALVILLE
EAST

SYSTON

BELGRAVE
& BIRSTALL

THURNBY

4
5
DESFORD 3 2 1 LEICESTER

N.JC.
CENT.JC.
WIGSTON
S.JC.

HINCKLEY

COUNTESTHORPE

MARKET
HARBOROUGH

LUTTERWORTH

LEICESTER STATIONS:
1. LONDON ROAD
2. CENTRAL
3. WEST BRIDGE
4. BELGRAVE ROAD
5. HUMBERSTONE ROAD

MIDLAND
GREAT CENTRAL
GREAT NORTHERN
LONDON & NORTH WESTERN
GN & LNW JT
LNW & MID JT

Introduction

Some years ago, a magazine was trying to find photos of Leicester's railways to accompany an article I had written. The editor was not having much luck; 'I've tried several photographers and they all say they never visited Leicester, but wish they had!'

The county has always been the Cinderella to both Nottingham and Derby (and that is not to impart that those two towns are Ugly Sisters!). In the 35 years I have known British railways, Leicestershire has never been an obvious Mecca, but there have been shifts of interest, with the lines around Nottingham losing much of their appeal or their existence, and Derby losing much importance with the downgrading of the Works and the severance, some years back, of the Midland main line to Manchester, through Matlock and the Peak District. Leicestershire, by contrast, has come more to the fore, with Coalville Open Days, the Great Central preservation movement, and Vic Berry. The latter, especially over the past five years or so, has become the flame that attracts hundreds of railway moths each year.

Photographers, now, can find much to interest them, despite the filling of the 'Leicester Gap', but there were always enthusiasts toting cameras. One of the biggest joys of preparing this book has been getting to know some of them. It took a little effort to find some of them, but they have totally disproved the above-mentioned editor's assertions; and the quality of their work has constantly surprised and delighted me.

Through this collection, I have tried to give a flavour of the county's railways and the way they have changed since Nationalisation in 1948, including pictures of some of the many things that have disappeared. In 1948 there were two main lines running north-south, together with distinctive branches from West Bridge, westwards to Desford (the pioneering Leicester-Swannington line), and the Great Northern at Belgrave Road, pushing eastwards for the trip to the coast; and there were five stations within the City boundaries. In addition, the county was criss crossed with all manner of other lines, either passing through, or branching within county parameters. Whilst not being totally inclusive, most of these are shown within the first four chapters. I have not included written histories of the lines, as these are more than adequately covered elsewhere and I have preferred to show the routes, taking an imaginary journey along them, rather than write about them. I hope I can awake and evoke some happy memories along the way. Chapter 5 detours away from the lines, but no book on the county would have been complete without a look at Brush and Vic Berry who, for opposing reasons, have been very important landmarks.

There are many who gave encouragement before the project reached the publishers and I extend my gratitude to these friends, but special mention must be made of the many photographers who made their work available for scrutiny. You can judge how much poorer this book would have been without them, but I have to offer real indebtedness and gratitude for their time and ever-ready help to the following: Geoff King, Horace Gamble, George Toms, Brian Morrison, Colin Marsden, Tom Heavyside, Roger Thwaites, David Richards, John Cooper-Smith, Ray Tilley. A very special debt is owed to: Chris Banks (for providing the key to a few doors); Derek Mercer (for putting up with constant bombardment of negatives and providing excellent results); Alec Ford (for his ready willingness to help, his courtesy and his overwhelming generosity); Neville Mays (for his kindness and accommodation at Brush and without whom Chapter 5 would have been impossible); Ray Green (for giving me artistic freedom); and my family – Judith, Adam and Tammy – for continually putting up with me burying my head in photos!

I have derived immense enjoyment in preparing this collection. I hope you derive as much from it.

M JOHN STRETTON
Spring 1989

1
Midland Main Line

1. *Above* At the time, this looked so ordinary, but signals, loco and coach have all now gone. At the south end of Market Harborough station, 45136 waits to re-start an 'up' express but, surprisingly, for Paddington not St Pancras, 25 August 1980.
TOM HEAVYSIDE

2. *Top right* In the good old days, when 'Jubilees' pulled *The Thames-Clyde Express* and spotters wore short trousers! The spotters' pent-up excitement can almost be felt, as 45659 *Drake* storms into Market Harborough station, on the 'up' train in September 1957.   RAY TILLEY

3. *Bottom right* The view from the bridge seen in Plate 2, looking back towards the station, on 12 April 1958, as 48369 (left) and 48365 (centre) prepare to pass, whilst 48757 (right) defies appearances and is involved in pushing before banking the train up the Northampton line.   RAY TILLEY

4. *Top* 48757 was frequently used on banking duties in the late Fifties at Market Harborough and is seen again, in 1957, awaiting the next turn, whilst (left) 49446 indulges in a bout of shunting. 49122 (centre) heads past with an 'up' freight, and (right) 48133 waits for its road to the north. RAY TILLEY

5. *Bottom* By 1964, not a lot had changed in this view of the same location from the other direction, but twenty years on only the main lines remained. On 19 September 1964 'Scot' 46155 *The Lancer* slows to a halt, before reversing to gain ex-LNWR territory, with the LCGB *Pennine Limited* special. GEOFF KING

6. *Right* Approaching Market Harborough from the north, 45126 slows with an 'up' express destined for St Pancras, 25 August 1980. TOM HEAVYSIDE

7. *Above* Brush Type 4s looked so much better in two-tone green and even in a black-and-white photo the difference can be seen on D1784, as it heads south between Kibworth and Market Harborough on an 'up' oil train, March 1978. JOHN COOPER-SMITH

8. *Left* In the days before HSTs, 'Peaks' held sway on the Midland main line and sights such as 45125, with its healthy rake of coaches, was a common sight. Heading south through Kibworth, bound for St Pancras, she is seen on 25 August 1980. TOM HEAVYSIDE

9. *Above* The 'down' relief line has obviously not seen much
recent traffic, judging by the drifts, whereas the main lines have
had the snow flattened. D129 looks attractive in the low sun,
leaving a fine powder curtain in its wake as it speeds through
Kibworth on a St Pancras-Leeds express, January 1969.
JOHN COOPER-SMITH

12. *Above* Past realignment of track at Wigston is clear (right) as
45148 approaches South Junction, at the head of 0900
St Pancras-Sheffield InterCity service, 26 March 1983.
BRIAN MORRISON

Two views of Wigston Magna station, sixteen years apart.

10. *Top left* With 'LMS' in cast letters still proudly emblazoned
on its bodyside, MR prototype diesel 10000 speeds through the
station in the bright sunshine of 20 March 1951, with the 1250
Leicester-St Pancras service. ALEC FORD

11. *Bottom left* Sixteen years on, the signals have moved position,
the buildings have detail differences and the station has a much
more delapidated appearance. On the last day of local services,
30 December 1967, the 1155 Leicester-Kettering DMU pauses
to pick up its complement of fresh passengers. MIKE MITCHELL

13. *Top* The origin of 44123 and 46400's train is shown on the smokebox door, as the returning holidaymakers, bound for Birmingham, take the spur to reach the line to Nuneaton at Wigston South Junction on 1 August 1953. Note that 44123 still has the 'British Railways' legend on its tender. ALEC FORD

14. *Bottom* Looking north, 48319 takes a leisurely route past Wigston South Junction on a long 'up' freight consisting mainly of coal, 22 August 1959. MIKE MENSING

Two more views of Wigston South Junction.

15. *Top right* During its extensive proving trials, the APT-E ran tests over the Midland main line. Looking for all the world like some bloated caterpillar, it heads for Leicester in May 1977. ROGER THWAITES

16. *Bottom right* Two years later, and there have been moves for track rationalisation and reclamation, especially from the carriage sidings, (upper left). The semaphores and signal box still have a few more years, though, as 45141 heads for St Pancras, 18 August 1979. TOM HEAVYSIDE

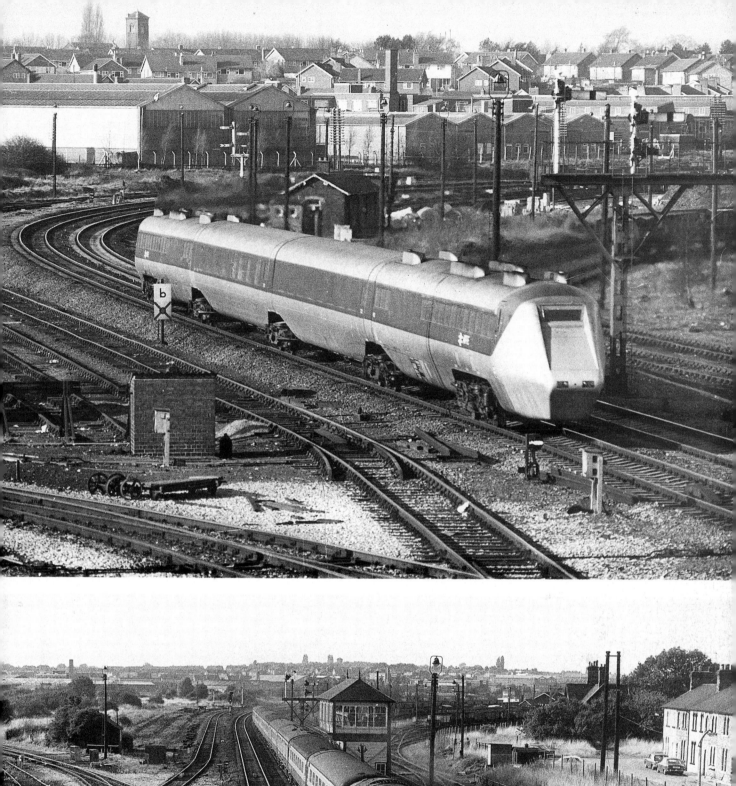

17. *Top* With three distinct junctions, Wigston was a very busy place in steam days and delights such as this beautifully clean 'Jubilee', 45669 *Fisher*, seen on a well mixed Leicester-Nuneaton freight, were not uncommon, 4 August 1962. BARRY HILTON

18. *Bottom* Representing twilight of steam in Leicestershire in more ways than one, 75039 runs light engine northwards, bound for Leicester shed, 17 December 1965. JOHN COOPER-SMITH

19. *Top* On 11 May 1963, 34006 *Bude* caused a real sensation in the county, heading the joint RCTS/LCGB North Midlands railtour. On the return journey she pauses in the late afternoon sun at Knighton South Junction curve in order to take water. GEOFF KING

20. *Bottom* Three years earlier, 43405 causes absolutely no stir, as she lazily shunts stock in the sidings between north, west and south junctions in 1960. ALEC FORD

Opposite

21. *Top left* The 'Garratts' were among my all-time favourite engines and although I only knew them briefly, I never ceased to enjoy watching them. Unusually, last-numbered 47999 is seen on the main line, about to take the Coalville/Burton line, having just passed through Knighton Tunnel, 10 August 1950.
ALEC FORD

22. *Bottom left* Closer to the tunnel mouth, 'Scot' 46142 *The York & Lancaster Regiment* bursts forth with an 'up' express, July 1960.
ALEC FORD

23. *Top* Just past Knighton Tunnel was Welford Road bridge and Cattle Market sidings. Passing the latter, 40138 of Nuneaton shed returns home with a mixed rake of stock, as the 1152 Leicester-Nuneaton (Trent Valley), in the late Fifties.
GEOFF KING

24. *Bottom* A very different and unusual view of the southern approaches to Leicester (London Road) station, sees an unidentified Sulzer (later Class 25) taking a rake of empty stock towards the platforms, as a sister engine heads the other way, around 1965. DAVID RICHARDS

25. *Top left* The midday St Pancras-Nottingham *Midland Pullman* reaches Leicester on 4 June 1963. Although diesel, the bright blue colouring always added glamour to sometimes drab surroundings.
GEOFF KING

26. *Bottom left* Almost twenty years on, and there are detail differences between tracks, the station has been cleaned and has lost its hoardings, but the greatest change has been the sweeping away of the buildings of Waterloo Street (upper left); now only the tree remains, as 45138 restarts the 1205 Nottingham-St Pancras on its way, 29 July 1982. CHRIS MILNER

27. *Top right* It is perhaps a little surprising that the facade of London Road station has remained largely untouched; but now cleaned up, as seen here on 5 April 1987, it makes for a very impressive advertisement for British Rail. The road layout, outside the station, has been drastically changed since this photograph.

28. *Bottom right* Inside the station, in steam days, there were station pilots, busy shunting coaching stock, or waiting to give aid wherever needed. Although it is into the early-Fifties, 1379 still has its pre-Nationalisation number and 'LMS' legend, as it shuffles about the snow at the southern end of the 'up' platforms. ALEC FORD

29. *Above* The flares and platform shoes give the game away for
the mid-Seventies. 47340 draws into Platform 1a of London
Road station with an unidentified service from St Pancras, 5 July
1975. TOM HEAVYSIDE

30. *Right* The all-over glass awning is well shown in this study of
light and shade, as 'Peak' 25 waits to restart the journey north,
with a St Pancras-Derby express, 4 August 1973.
JOHN COOPER-SMITH

Before and after modernisation of London Road.

31. *Top left* Although the inner parts of the trainshed tended to be murky, at least the architecture had style, and after the smoky glass was removed it had much more light. It also seemed big and important, as can be seen from this view of 45126, framed by the end canopies, as it stands awaiting the green light for the 1725 St Pancras-Derby, 5 July 1975. TOM HEAVYSIDE

32. *Bottom left* By contrast the 'modern' station looks far less imposing or attractive, and is much breezier! An immaculate 47545 pauses for a crew change, whilst hauling ecs of the Royal Train, bound for Sheffield, 15 March 1984. CHRIS MILNER

33. *Above* A truly emotive picture for those who knew Leicester. The buildings and cross signals (left) and the light, shed buildings and Midland signal (right) all long-since gone. The whole picture oozes lost atmosphere, as 'Jubilee' 45573 *Newfoundland* breezes into London Road station with an express bound for St Pancras, 14 August 1950. ALEC FORD

34. *Top* One of the often frustrating but equally intriguing and, in hindsight, amazing things about railways in Britain is the constant and seemingly inexorable change. In the area framed by bridge and platform of London Road station in this picture, virtually the only things left which relate to the railway are the rails and the lampstandards. Reporting codes disappeared many years ago, the signals during the closing of the 'Leicester Gap', and the buildings on the left around the same time. 45124 lasted until January 1988, but not on the kind of service seen on 5 July 1975, as the 1430 Blackpool-Leicester arrives at its destination.
TOM HEAVYSIDE

35. *Bottom* 'Peaks' were ousted by HSTs, represented here by 43111, trying hard to emulate its steam ancestors, as it restarts the 0835 St Pancras-Sheffield out of London Road station, 1 January 1989.

Opposite

36. *Top* In the heady days when steam seemed forever, an unidentified Standard Class 5 adds to the general smoky atmosphere, resting between duties on Leicester Midland (15C) shed, 4 June 1957.

37. *Bottom* In the days when the Birdcage was Mecca, hours would be spent viewing the many and ever-changing locos on shed, such as 46403, 46454, 45264, 40135, 44278, 44962 and 46420 seen here, 9 April 1960.

38. *Top left* By 1984 things had changed dramatically, but the shed was still busy, as can be seen from the number of engines surrounding the very rare visitors, electrics 82004 and 82006, en route to Vic Berry's yard, 30 September 1984.

39. *Bottom left* Four years later and the scene is again very different. Now the passenger duties have been lost to the shed, more of the yard is a repository for Vic Berry and the weeds evidence some dereliction. (Left to right) 47222 *Appleby-Frodingham*, 56064, L102, 46023 and 25080. The latter somehow reached Leicester and then was banned further movement, as it was missing a buffer! 1 January 1989.

40. *Top* On the turntable of the shed roundhouse, 47441 is shunted by a sister 'Jinty', 13 April 1958.

41. *Bottom* By 2 March 1963 the low evening sun casts shadows over the turntable pit and a much different scene, as D5409 is re-fuelled. Having travelled to Scotland, becoming 27116, 27210 and finally 27064 along the way, it ironically returned to Leicester in 1987 to Vic Berry's for scrapping! ROGER THWAITES

42. *Top left* With smoke and dust being blown around in a strong wind, 42940 and 'Jubilee' 45689 *Ajax* stand in the corner of the shed yard, by the small works building, 2 March 1963. ROGER THWAITES

43. *Bottom left* By 1 January 1989, all that remains of the same view is one track and the embankment! 08697 enjoys the peace of the New Year before being called on again.

44. *Top right* First station out of Leicester going north, Humberstone Road was closed in the mid-Sixties, but was once one of five stations within the city boundaries. In happier days, 45333 speeds north with a *City of Leicester Midland Holiday Express* – destination unknown – just before midday, 11 August 1960. GEOFF KING

45. *Bottom right* Perhaps because of their uncommon appearance, and the lack of front number right through to the end, 'Duck 8s' were always a welcome sight. 49444 ambles an 'up' freight towards Humberstone Road in August 1959. ALEC FORD

46. *Top* A lack of urgency is obvious from the sight of 48370 as it slowly plods south to Leicester shed, past Ashwell & Nesbit works, on the northern outskirts of the city, July 1962.

47. *Bottom* Another 8F, 48149, works south, on revenue-earning service this time, passing the workmen's hut at Thurmaston on a hot summer's afternoon, August 1960.

48. *Top* Where I spent literally hours trainspotting. Once a common sight and now only a fond memory, 'Crab' 42756 works hard with a full train of coal, heading for Leicester on a dull winter's day through Thurmaston, 5 February 1960.

49. *Bottom* In their heyday, we saw double-headed 'Metrovicks' every day on the Condor freight, but they were rarer on passenger duties. D5705 (now preserved) leads sister D5711 on a Manchester-St Pancras express, as the sun peers through the mist of 5 February 1960.

Two views of the same place, and the same bridge as seen in the background of the last two plates.

50. *Top* In the summer of 1961, 45667 *Jellicoe* is not overworked at the head of an early morning Nottingham-Leicester local train. GEOFF KING

51. *Bottom* By 20 June 1982, as 45122 gathers speed with the 1200 Sheffield-St Pancras service, the signal and trappings have gone, the telegraph poles seem to have been eaten(!), and the undergrowth has developed. Within five years, HSTs will have taken over and the double goods track reduced to single.

Opposite

52. *Top* From the bridge of the last two plates, looking north towards Syston, 45040 is seen on test from Derby Works, double-headed with 47462 on a southbound vans train, 18 May 1984. COLIN MARSDEN

53. *Bottom* Looking back from Syston station bridge, 31114 is framed by a variety of signalling as it hauls the 1505 Birmingham (New Street)-Cambridge, 26 March 1983. BRIAN MORRISON

54. *Top left* The end is not far away, as can be judged from the fact that 'Sandringham' 61660 *Hull City* has lost her nameplates, as she starts the first stopper of the day from Peterborough-Leicester at around 0930, out of Syston station, 8 April 1960. GEOFF KING

55. *Centre left* The drowsy feel and nature of many suburban stations can be felt from this view of 40104 and 78028, as they pause at Syston station, en route for Loughborough, where they will separate to run early-evening locals back to Leicester, 28 June 1957. GEOFF KING

56. *Bottom left* Another 'Sandringham', 61657 *Doncaster Rovers*, this time with nameplates, takes a breather at Syston at the head of the 1615 Leicester-Peterborough in 1959. DAVID RICHARDS

Opposite

57. *Top right* With the loading gauge and Midland Railway notice betraying origins, Syston station plays temporary host to 46502 of Nottingham shed, hauling a Nottingham-Leicester local, August 1956. GEOFF KING

58. *Bottom right* The signal gantry (above), just to the north of the station, was a longtime landmark but this, together with sidings and platforms, has been swept away by 26 March 1983, as 45119 heads the 1600 Derby-St Pancras southwards. BRIAN MORRISON

59. *Top* For a long time, the land in the triangle formed by Syston's northern junctions held carriage sidings. In those days, 'Jubilee' 45618 *New Hebrides* hauls empty stock southwards towards Leicester, under Syston's famed gantry, prior to forming a Leicester-Paignton Saturday extra, 4 August 1962.
GEOFF KING

60. *Bottom* The view from the other side of the gantry, as consecutively numbered D5185 and D5184, together with short-lived brake tender, drag a weird mixture of wagons northwards in the early morning of 27 July 1963. GEOFF KING

61. *Above* In the months preceding closure in 1987, Syston North Junction signal box was an oft-visited location. On 1 March 1987, a mere five weeks before closure and six weeks before demolition, history is still intact inside the box, showing how much has been lost and thrown away.

62. *Top left* Outside the box, the appealing set of semaphores and trackwork can readily be seen, as HST power car 43106 leads the 1510 Nottingham-St Pancras southwards, 26 March 1983.
BRIAN MORRISON

63. *Bottom left* Colour light signals now replace the semaphores and the trackwork has been rationalised, as 58015 waits by these new signals in the mist of 30 April 1988, viewed from the signalbox bridge.

64. *Top right* HST power car 43058 leads the 1015 St Pancras-Nottingham, through the mist near Cossington, 30 April 1988.

65. *Bottom right* Looking the other way, 20169 and 20044 haul an 'up' mixed goods past Cossington, 8 September 1981, again through the mist. COLIN MARSDEN

Opposite

66. *Top left* The fireman of 58142 has obviously earned a rest, as the 2F gets to grips with a heavily loaded southbound freight at Barrow-upon-Soar, 30 June 1951. ALEC FORD

67. *Bottom left* Gangers exchange brief words with the driver of 45136, which has just brought ballast from Loughborough. Barrow-upon-Soar, 5 November 1986. COLIN MARSDEN

68. *Top right* In the very last days of steam on the Midland, 48349 seems an unusual presence on the main line, with a very mixed bunch of freight vehicles. The fireman has presumably just fed the boiler with dubious quality coal, judging by the colour of the smoke, but he prefers to look back to where he has just come from, south of Loughborough, 22 August 1965. JOHN COOPER-SMITH

69. *Bottom right* Where it all started for me as a schoolboy collecting train numbers, Loughborough station shows much of its original Midland construction as 45054 pulls in with the 1035 Derby-St Pancras, Sunday 6 July 1975. TOM HEAVYSIDE

Opposite

70. *Top left* 44004 *Great Gable* certainly looks in no hurry as she moves an engineer's train into Loughborough station, 6 July 1975. Some of the vast expanse of Brush Engineering's Works can be seen (right). TOM HEAVYSIDE

71. *Bottom left* Just a few minutes earlier, the torpor of a hot summer Sunday is almost tangible in this view of *Great Gable*, shunting in the engineers' sidings just north of Loughborough station, 6 July 1975. TOM HEAVYSIDE

72. *Top* Approaching the northern limits of the county, double-headed 'Rats' 25212 and 25299 head an unidentified 'up' train, at Normanton-on-Soar, 5 July 1975. TOM HEAVYSIDE

73. *Bottom* The coal merry-go-round trains have earned vast sums for BR. En route from Silverhill to Northfleet, 56054 is on such a duty, 28 June 1983. COLIN MARSDEN

2
Great Central

74. *Top* Lutterworth was the southernmost station in the county and tended to be overlooked by photographers. A rare view of the station's signal box is seen behind 'Hall' 6929 *Whorlton Hall* of Banbury shed, at the head of the 1720 Leicester Central-Woodford Halse, viewed from a carriage of the 1705 reverse train, Tuesday, 25 July 1961. HORACE GAMBLE

75. *Bottom* One of the reasons for the decline of the Great Central was the proliferation of cars and the building of the M1 motorway. The latter can be seen (left) as 73004 leaves Lutterworth station, heading north with the 1438 Marylebone-Nottingham Victoria semi-fast, 22 May 1965. MIKE MENSING

Opposite

76. *Top right* Stalwarts of GC freights before and after Nationalisation, and even into the days of Standard 9Fs, were LNER 2-8-0s. O1 63773 does not look unduly worried by its load on the climb towards Lutterworth with an 'up' freight, 12 September 1956. MIKE MENSING

77. *Bottom right* *The South Yorkshireman* was for many years *the* crack express on the GC, and A3s the stars. 60059 *Tracery* has been graced with a very mixed rake of coaches for the 'up' train of 12 September 1956, working hard, despite outward appearances, against the gradient two miles north of Lutterworth. MIKE MENSING

78. *Top* The Standard Class 9Fs most often travelled at leisurely pace, hauling coal freights backwards and forwards, but here 92153 has really got the bit between its teeth as it approaches Ashby Tunnel with an 'up' freight, 9 May 1964. BARRY HILTON

79. *Bottom* In the mid-Sixties English Electric Type 3s were drafted into the Central to try to save money on the running costs of the Nottingham-Marylebone trains. They saw mixed service and here D6815, looking in very fine condition, heads south with Leicester City supporters, for the Cup Final match against Manchester City, 25 May 1963. BARRY HILTON

80. *Top right* Standard Class 5s were also drafted in to help improve services. 73053 appears to have steam to spare as she leaves the A426 road-bridge behind, heading the 1625 Marylebone-Nottingham, 1½ miles north of Ashby Magna, 3 June 1961. MIKE MENSING

81. *Bottom right* During the Sixties, the lion's share of freight work did fall more and more to the 9Fs. The loads were varied and 92010 has worked much harder than shown here, with this payload of steel bars, north of Ashby Magna, 3 June 1961. MIKE MENSING

82. *Top left* For a few brief months in 1961 the line was graced and brightened by the appearance of prototype Gas Turbine loco GT3. Towards the end of its stay, on 21 September, the engine enters Ashby Magna station on an unidentified 'down' train, possibly on test, from Marylebone-Nottingham. MIKE MENSING

83. *Centre* B1s were ever-present on the GC, but never too frequently to outstay their appeal. 61041 looks in really fine shape as she hauls an 'up' Cup Final special, bound for Wembley, 2 May 1959. BARRY HILTON

84. *Bottom left* K3s were another popular class on the line. 61838 has obviously seen some hard work, necessitating the repainting of part of the smokebox door, as she speeds south with a Newcastle-Cardiff express out of Dunton Bassett Tunnel, 29 August 1959 BARRY HILTON

85. *Top left* Yet another light load for a 9F! 92070 heads south with ballast near Whetstone, 27 September 1958.
BARRY HILTON

Two views of Leicester, Marlow Road.

86. *Centre* In the days when locals were locals, Leicester Central (15E) shed's own 42453 heads south with the 1235 service to Rugby, 18 August 1962. BARRY HILTON

87. *Bottom right* Whilst the Midland had to make do with mundane 'Black Fives' for its holiday specials, the GC borrowed 61665 *Leicester City* for the week! On 14 August 1956 she accelerates away from the environs of Leicester with a London-bound excursion. GEOFF KING

Opposite

88. *Top left* Another B1 hard at work on passenger duty, 61201 heads a Manchester-Marylebone express towards Marlow Road, 20 September 1958. BARRY HILTON

89. *Bottom left* A handful of usually Banbury-allocated 'Halls' were common sights on the GC metals to Leicester and one of them, 4924 *Eydon Hall*, having worked north on the Bournemouth-York service, enjoys the early evening sunshine of 23 May 1958, passing Leicester South Goods yard with the 'up' fish from Grimsby. GEOFF KING

90. *Top* Another 9F, this time on a real train! The heavy train is making 92076 work hard as she passes Leicester South Goods and the road into the Central shed (right), 12 April 1958. BARRY HILTON

91. *Bottom* One of the regulars on *The South Yorkshireman* and one of my real favourites, A3 60111 *Enterprise*, still in original condition, without the German Federal smoke deflectors fitted later, passing Leicester South Goods, with a Manchester-Marylebone express, 15 June 1957. GEOFF KING

92. *Top left* Leicester Central (38C/15E) was a classic GC shed and this is a classic shot. LNER workhorses and railmen in 'workhorse' uniforms; 63796 receives attention from her driver whilst his mate prepares to climb back into the cab, and 60890 rests temporarily on home shed, Monday, 16 July 1962. HORACE GAMBLE

93. *Centre* An extremely rare shot, Southern Region B4 0-4-0T *Jersey* stands at the side of Leicester Central shed in 1949, although the reason for the visit and where she was going to/coming from is a mystery. ALEC FORD

94. *Bottom left* The J10s were also not frequent visitors to the Central shed and 65158 would not have been here, except for running a hot box, en route from Woodford Halse-Gorton for scrapping, Saturday 7 May 1960. HORACE GAMBLE

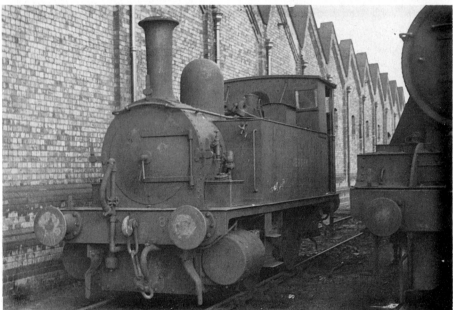

Opposite

95. A picture that says it all about some of the less welcome weather conditions. The sky is heavy with more snow, which fell again shortly after this photo was taken, showing driver and mate turning the hard way, but no doubt keeping warm doing it! 61350 just fits the turntable, during the very bad winter of 1963. DAVID RICHARDS

96. *Top left* In a picture that is saturated in nostalgic interest, 44847 leaves the Leicester Central station area and passes the carriage sheds (left) at the head of a Bank Holiday excursion to London, 6 August 1962. GEOFF KING

97. *Bottom left* Two decades or so later and the remains of Vic Berry's infamous pile (middle distance) is roughly where 44847 was in Plate 96! The footpath (Leicester Corporation's 'Great Central Way'!) straddles the ex-'down' (left) and 'up' main lines and the motorbike provides a totally different sort of power. To the right, through the arch, is Berry's site, 1 January 1989.

Opposite

98. A very dramatic and atmospheric view of 92124 gathering speed into the mist, heading light engine for Leicester Central shed, past the Leicester South Passenger signalbox, 28 November 1964.
JOHN COOPER-SMITH

100. *Above* Three distinct types of motive power congregate at the south end of Leicester Central station, around 1960. (Left to right) B1 61063, 'Jubilee' 45739 *Ulster* and K3 61972, represent Thompson, Stanier and Gresley, three very different schools of design thought. GEOFF KING

Opposite

99. In much happier days, when the Great Central was still a vibrant line, regular GC A3 performer 60102 *Sir Frederick Banbury* of Leicester Central (38C) shed, restarts a Manchester-Marylebone express from Leicester at around 1130, 14 August 1950. ALEC FORD

Then and then!

101. *Top left* Always welcome visitors to Leicester on cross-region workings, 'Halls' gave nice variety: 6970 *Whaddon Hall* looks in great shape to haul a Banbury-bound train, from the Central station in 1962. ALEC FORD

102. *Bottom left* Within seven years, things had changed dramatically. No longer any steam and the trackwork drastically cut back, the station has a distinctly forlorn feeling as the 1617 Nottingham Arkwright Street-Rugby leaves on the last day of services, 3 May 1969. BARRY HILTON

Opposite

103. *Top right* 44846 seems to be making heavy weather of shunting a few vans in the sidings of Leicester Central station, 23 August 1964. JOHN COOPER-SMITH

104. *Bottom right* The building (right) is that seen behind 44846 in Plate 103, but how everything else has changed! Now, factory units stand (left) where the station platforms were – a sad end for a once proud railway, Leicester Central, 2 January 1983.

105. *Top left* 44780 eases off the regulator, the hard work climbing the bank (left distance) having been completed, entering Leicester Central station, with the 1730 Nottingham Victoria-Marylebone, *c*1965. DAVID RICHARDS

106. *Bottom left* Immediately to the north of Leicester Central station, the line crossed the River Soar at the quaintly named Frog Island. On a misty day, when the steam from the factory (right) hovers close to the water's surface, an unidentified 9F hauls an empty coal train northwards in 1960. DAVID RICHARDS

Opposite

107. *Top right* Northwards out of Leicester, the GC climbed all the way to Birstall, 'Britannia' 70014 *Iron Duke* gets to grips with a Marylebone-Nottingham semi-fast, past Abbey Lane sidings, 4 August 1962. GEOFF KING

108. *Bottom right* The very cold conditions make for most attractive smoke effects from 44847, midway through the climb up Birstall bank, on a Rugby-Nottingham Victoria local, January 1963. GEOFF KING

Opposite

109. *Top left* 9Fs were usually exclusively used on freights, but in emergencies were pressed into passenger work, and often equipped themselves with merit. 92154 climbs Birstall bank in fine style, leaving Leicester with a northbound special for Skegness, August 1964. GEOFF KING

110. *Bottom left* At the top of the bank, approaching Belgrave & Birstall station, 'Halls' were rare venturers north of Leicester, but for around twelve months in the early mid-Sixties, they worked regularly through to Nottingham. 7910 *Hown Hall* is pressing on for that city with a northbound inter-regional special in 1964. GEOFF KING

111. *Above* The more normal view of the southern approach to Belgrave & Birstall station, with V2 60878 of York shed heading north with a fitted freight, probably the returning 'Hull Fish' breasting the 1 in 176 climb, 31 August 1961. GEOFF KING

112. *Above* The view looking the other way to Plate 111. There are not many takers for the golf course (left), but the snow makes the scene very attractive in the sun, as 92093 shuffles southwards with a coal train, 19 January 1963. GEOFF KING

113. *Bottom left* After closure in the early Sixties, until closure of the line in 1969, Belgrave & Birstall station was kept in good repair, with occasional weeding of platforms, etc. Into the Seventies, damage by vandals and dereliction became more frequent and marked, to the extent that, by 27 December 1982, the place was positively unsafe. Sadly, although the preserved Great Central was to reach this station by 1988, these buildings had had to be swept away.

Opposite
Before and after

114. *Top right* In the early Sixties, this scene seemed so permanent. 92012 passes Belgrave & Birstall station with a 'down' coal empties train, when closure never entered the heads of us young spotters. 14 August 1962. LES WADE

115. *Bottom right* Hardly recognisable as the same location! Nature is doing its best to retake the cutting, as a young Adam Stretton views where tracks used to be, but is too young to remember them personally. Happily, by 1988, the track was back under the arch. 31 May 1986.

116. *Top left* Another view of a 9F on passenger duty. 92132 brings a Skegness-Leicester (Central) excursion southwards, including a Gresley coach still finding employment, approaching Belgrave & Birstall station from the north in 1964. GEOFF KING

117. *Bottom left* The housing estate to the north of Belgrave & Birstall station had a good view of the line. 64453 with a very mixed rake of freight vehicles bound for Leicester, ex-Nottingham, 24 April 1957. GEOFF KING

118. *Top right* Unusually for the mid-Fifties, a 'Black Five' deputises for an A3 on the 'down' *South Yorkshireman*. 44912 is seen with a complete rake of 'blood-and-custard' coaches, between Birstall and Rothley. GEOFF KING

119. *Bottom right* One of the delights in the later years of local services from Nottingham Victoria-Leicester Central was the evening stopper deploying the ex-GC 'Directors'. In the twilight of her years, 62664 *Princess Mary* drifts down the gradient towards Birstall at approx. 2030, the train having originated at Sheffield (Victoria), 9 July 1958. GEOFF KING

120. No portrait of the Great Central would be complete
without views of the preservation work and, specifically, *Duke
of Gloucester*. Despite all the doubting Thomases, and against
all the odds, 71000 has been successfully and magnificently
rebuilt and is seen here, in immaculate condition, pulling out of
Rothley station on the 1505 train to Loughborough, 12 April
1987. JOHN COOPER-SMITH

The variety of preserved motive power on the railway is quite diverse, as will be seen from the next few shots.

121. *Top* LNER 4744 has been a stalwart of the line ever since its arrival, and at times has been the real mainstay of services. Yet another successful trip reaches the terminus at Rothley, 4 March 1979. ROGER THWAITES

122. *Bottom* Affectionately known as 'Teddy Bears', the ex-BR Class 14s D9523 and D9516 have also given good and reliable service. On a special Diesel Weekend, they haul the first train of the day, the 1130 Loughborough-Rothley, past Swithland reservoir and the proposed site of Swithland station, never built. 30 October 1982.

123. *Top* Although somewhat artificial, an attempted evocation by the preserved Great Central Railway (GCR) of a freight in original GC days, seen between Rothley and Quorn, heading south towards Rothley, near Swithland, 3 March 1979.
ROGER THWAITES

124. *Bottom* During the Diesel Weekend of 30 October 1982, GCR staged a mail pick-up at speed, using preserved 'Director' 506 *Butler Henderson*. In very poor weather conditions, the train can be seen roaring through Quorn, about to catch the pouch. *See p.80 for captions to p.79.*

Previous page

125. *Top* Showing just what sort of standards are being achieved by the preservation movement, 'Black Five' 5231, now named *3rd (Volunteer) Battalion The Worcestershire and Sherwood Foresters Regiment*, and supposedly allocated to 16A Nottingham(!), pauses at Quorn, 11 March 1979. ROGER THWAITES

126. *Bottom* Another 'Black Five', this time in reality in BR days, 44920 heads south out of Loughborough, making fine shadows on the embankment in the early evening sunshine of June 1966, in the last few months of steam on the line, with a Nottingham Victoria-Marylebone semi-fast. JOHN COOPER-SMITH

127. *Top left* Captured by Brush Engineering's official photographer, D5637 is on trial on the GC, being used on the Bournemouth-York inter-regional service, pausing at Loughborough Central station, 4 October 1961. BEM

128. *Bottom left* One more example of brilliant preservation work. The gleaming 'coat' of 506 *Butler Henderson* (the only preserved ex-GC loco) gets due attention at Loughborough, just outside the shed area, 12 April 1982. JOHN COOPER-SMITH

1. *Top* In the days when Wigston South Junction was a busy place and locals still ran to various points of the compass, 43042 passes the Junction with the 1720 Leicester (London Road)-Bedford stopper, 22 August 1959. MIKE MENSING

2. *Bottom* A true view of the latter days of steam on the Midland, when the engines were more than not in disgraceful condition and the weather was less than good. 'Jubilee' 45573 *Newfoundland* passes under Welford Road bridge, on the way south out of Leicester with a four-coach local in 1965. DAVID RICHARDS

3. *Top* The view through an HST cab window, at the north end of Leicester (London Road) station, showing much of the 'old' railway that has since been swept away and, somewhat unusually, a Class 37 on shed (right), 28 May 1986.

4. *Bottom* The late spring evening sun gives an unnatural cast to the view of 08618 and 08695, on Leicester depot, 18 April 1982. The difference in condition could hardly be more marked and it is interesting to note the difference in front-end warning markings and the lack of class information transfer on 08695.

5. *Top* Adding a touch of colour to Leicester depot on 31 May 1987, 58042 *Ironbridge Power Station* stands in the company of 56061.

6. *Bottom* Steam had officially finished on the Midland by this time, but standing alone at approx. 0830 on 10 September 1966, it was easy to wallow in nostalgia as 4472 *Flying Scotsman*, beautifully restored, passes near Thurmaston on the outward leg of a special.

7. *Top* *Flying Scotsman* was the cause of the crowd (right) getting a little agitated at the 9F and its train, as the special, with *Scotsman* at the head, was then due. Barkby Thorpe, 9 May 1965.

8. *Bottom* By the late Eighties, HSTs ruled. Having undergone more than one livery change, 43051 *The Duke & Duchess of York* and its train are in the latest swallow InterCity colours, forming the 0835 St Pancras-Sheffield, seen passing near Thurmaston, 7 August 1988.

9. *Top* D6749 hauls the daily Bournemouth-York inter-regional train away from Lutterworth, 22 May 1965, in an attempt to cut costs and save the GC from run-down and closure, also competing with the M1 motorway (left). MIKE MENSING

10. *Bottom* 'Jubilee' 45598 *Basutoland* of Burton shed is a strange visitor to the GC, emerging from Ashby Magna Tunnel at the head of a First Class only Cup Final special, taking Leicester City fans to Wembley, 25 May 1963. BARRY HILTON

11. *Top* A near-timeless view of a scene of recreation by the preserved GCR, as *Littleton No. 5* stands at Quorn station in the late afternoon sunshine, in the autumn of 1974.

12. *Bottom* The immaculate condition of 71000 *Duke of Gloucester* after restoration is testament to the hundreds of hours of sheer hard work put in by the volunteers, transforming it to working condition from that as seen in the mid-Seventies. at Loughborough.

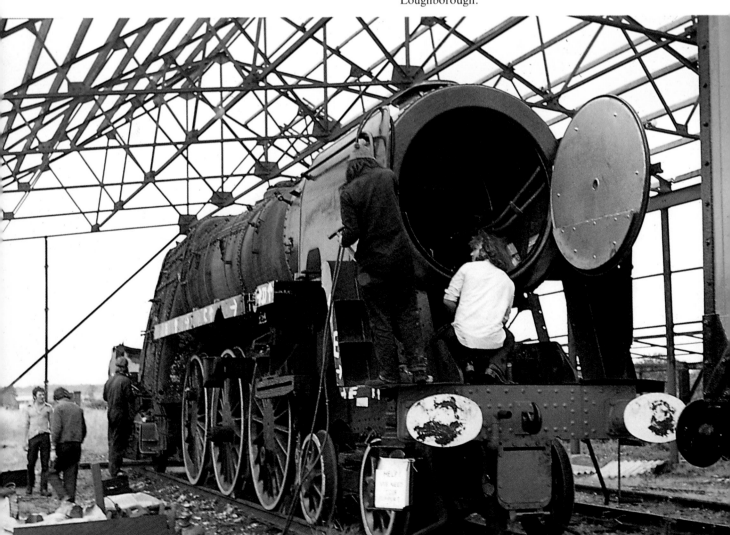

13. *Top* Colour shots of the West Bridge branch are rare, as are the details of this shot of 58148 at Glenfield!

14. *Bottom* One could almost imagine that trains still ran over the viaduct at Tilton in the delightful east-Leicestershire countryside shown here in September 1973, but the tracks have long been ripped up from the ex-GN&LNW Joint line.

15. *Top* Preparing to take the branch to Nuneaton, unrebuilt 'Patriot' 45537 *Private E Sykes VC* is a rare visitor to the Midland line, especially on freight duties, and more especially in such immaculate condition. Wigston North Junction, 4 March 1961. BARRY HILTON

16. *Bottom* Having been stripped of asbestos, D212 (also carrying numbers 40012 and 97407) stands next to the emerging third paint shed at Vic Berry's, ready to be taken to a new life in preservation, 30 October 1988.

3
West Bridge and
Great Northern

129. *Top left* Some of the land that was once taken up by the West Bridge terminus of the original Leicester-Swannington Railway. Equally ancient in its way, 58298 shunts a variety of trucks used on a Leicester Railway Society guard's van visit to the line, at the terminus, 14 June 1958. BARRY HILTON

130. *Bottom left* In the last days of the line, BR Standard 78028, with cutdown cab, has displaced the more elderly motive power and shunts, somewhat unusually, stone wagons at West Bridge on a dismal day in March 1966, just weeks before the end.
DAVID RICHARDS

131. *Top right* A truly idyllic railway photograph. The setting is ideal: peaceful, with the proliferation of rosebay willow herb, bramble, and trees. The diminutive 58148 looks delightful as it brings its train of brakevanned enthusiasts out of Glenfield Tunnel during the joint SLS/MLS *Leicestershire Railtour*, 8 September 1962. GEOFF KING

132. *Bottom right* Glenfield Tunnel, with its very restricted height, was the reason for the very small locos on the line, and the cause of the cut-down cab of 78028, seen leaving the tunnel in June 1964 with a goods train for Desford. Note that the undergrowth has developed a little since the above picture. GEOFF KING

133. *Top left* Glenfield Tunnel can again be seen in the background, as push-pull fitted 41321 waits while its passengers stretch their legs during the Leicester Railway Society's *21st Anniversary Special*, 27 May 1961. HORACE GAMBLE

134. *Centre* An LRS trip of earlier vintage has line-regular 58298 at the helm, pausing during the brakevan trip of 14 June 1958. BARRY HILTON

135. *Bottom left* Another view of the *21st Anniversary Special* of 27 May 1961, this time pausing at Glenfield station. BARRY HILTON

136. *Top right* By June 1964 the station at Glenfield looks decidedly unkempt, with edging stones being progressively removed, as 78028 enters the station with the 1200 freight from West Bridge. GEOFF KING

137. *Centre* The LRS trip of 14 June 1958 goes over the road crossing at Glenfield on its return journey, past the delightfully shaped crossing house. BARRY HILTON

138. *Bottom right* The progress of the 1200 West Bridge-Desford freight is further monitored, as 78028 crosses the road at Glenfield, June 1964. GEOFF KING

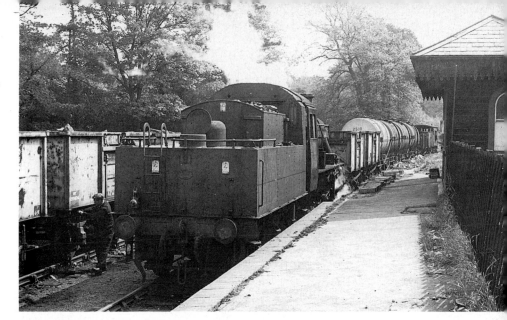

Opposite

139. *Top left* Another delightful rural scene. Although the passenger service had long been withdrawn between West Bridge and Desford, the freight duties were still many at the date of this view. With the 'LMS' legend still very visible on the tender, 58247 passes an early caravan site on the approach to Ratby station, with the crew very keen to get into the shot! 7 April 1952. ALEC FORD

140. *Bottom left* Just a minute or two later, and 58247 and crew have gone over the road crossing and have reached Ratby station itself. ALEC FORD

141. *Top right* By June 1964 the loop had gone (see plate 139), as had the LMS poster board on the goods shed wall, and the crossing gates had been slewed to an angle. The 1200 from West Bridge is seen slowly making its way towards Desford. GEOFF KING

142. *Centre* Out into the country between Ratby and Desford, 58148, with the working's number prominently displayed, nears journey's end with the 1200 West Bridge-Desford freight, 27 July 1963. GEOFF KING

143. *Bottom right* The same scene four year earlier, with a tree top crow's nest and the signal post with a different coat, as 58209, with the old-style cab and protection sheet, trundles towards Desford, 11 April 1959. BARRY HILTON

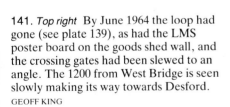

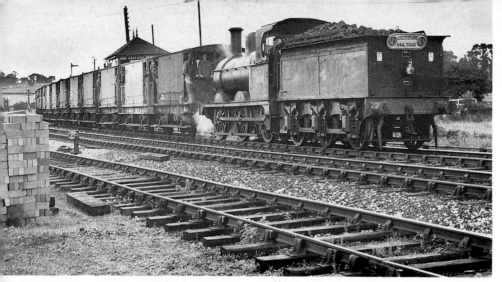

144. *Top left* The joint SLS/MLS *Leicestershire Railtour* starts on its way to Leicester, past the goods yard at Desford, behind 58148, 8 September 1962. GEOFF KING

145. *Centre* In the last days of these 2Fs controlling the branch, 58182 (last of the class and withdrawn just four months later) backs across the road at Desford, 14 September 1963. Standard Class 2s took over from November 1963. BARRY HILTON

146. *Bottom left* A typical view of a branch line in summer sun with a feeling of peace and relaxation. 58148 pauses between shunting at Desford, 27 July 1963. GEOFF KING

Opposite

147. *Top right* The original intention of the Great Northern Railway was to drive its line across the city of Leicester, but it only got as far as Belgrave Road station, which was a terminus built on the grand scale. Some of this grandeur can be seen around 61088 as she stands in the dappled sunlight, 1 September 1962, having brought in the 1318 ex-Skegness train. The last of the infamous east coast holiday excursion trains from this station ran one week later. BARRY HILTON

148. *Bottom right* The interest and fascination of boys with railways is obvious from these three, giving the 'once-over' to 61763 and 61056, both having brought in excursions from the coast, 17 August 1957. RAY TILLEY

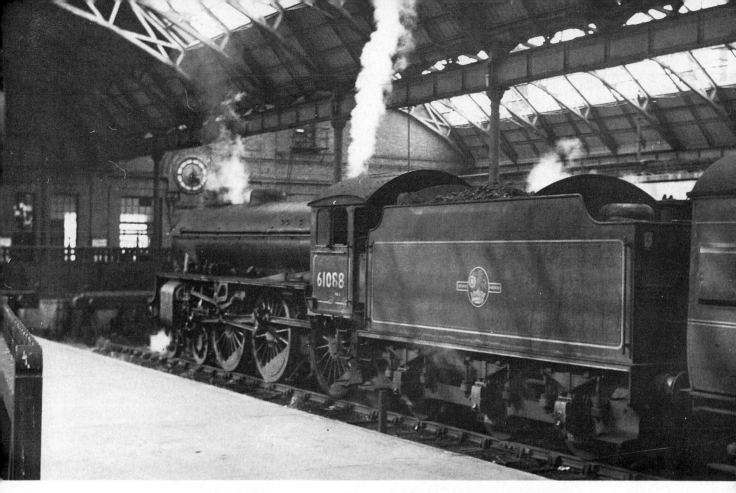

149. *Top left* A truly classic view of Belgrave Road station with literally everything in view now gone, even the houses on the left. On 11 April 1952, however, the picture is very much different: 64249 simmering quietly (left) as 64200, double-headed with 64257, waits to pull away with a Skegness excursion. Note the antiquated stock (right) and the many detail difference in the two signal gantries. ALEC FORD

150. *Bottom left* The weeds are beginning to show and an air of some dereliction is creeping into the scene (see plate 149), as 61142 waits to take the long road to the sea on my eighteenth birthday, 3 August 1961. GEOFF KING

151. *Top* After the station was closed and demolished, the goods shed was used as a warehouse. 'Railway Goods Depot' can still just be made out above the large 'Premier' sign on 11 March 1984 but, then the only remaining evidence of the once large complex, it succumbed two years after this view to become the site for a Sainsbury's hypermarket.

152. *Bottom* Our means of transport can be seen leaning against the lamp-post, as 61209 reaches its destination with its load of ex-Mablethorpe holidaymakers, Saturday, 29 July 1961. DAVID RICHARDS

153. The site of the station on 11 March 1984, with the goods depot (left). A clump of bushes (middle distance) has replaced 61209 and the bridge and signalbox have disappeared under the houses (middle right). The site is now a toys' warehouse!

Two views of Catherine Street bridge.

154. A rare view of a 'Black Five' at Belgrave Road. 45238 reverses the RCTS *East Midlands Branch Rail Tour* out of the platforms, under the bridge, May 1963. GEOFF KING

155. A class commonly used on freights on the branch in happier times, J39 64804 gathers speed away from the bridge, past the delightful somersault signal, on an afternoon (SO) goods selection bound for Colwick, 3 September 1960. GEOFF KING

Opposite

156. *Top right* A very rare shot of Leicester (GN) shed (sub to Colwick). Equally rare to those of us who started trainspotting in the mid-Fifties were J5s, of which class 65007 stands in the evening sunshine, 24 March 1951. One of the first of the class to be withdrawn, she went in February 1952. ALEC FORD

157. *Bottom right* The road into the GN shed can be seen (right) as 61141 brings yet another train from Skegness towards the destination of Belgrave Road, 3 September 1960. GEOFF KING

158. *Top left* B1 61281 has a heavy load to take back to Colwick(!), climbing from Forest Road with an empty brakevan in the early morning sunshine of summer 1961, past a classic somersault signal. GEOFF KING

159. *Bottom left* Having brought the holidaymakers safely home, 61773 climbs the bank to Humberstone station with the empty twelve-coach train bound for Colwick, 9 August 1958. GEOFF KING

160. *Top right* Proudly displaying the 38A Colwick shed plate and looking in fine condition, 61283 breasts the bank near Thurnby with a Belgrave Road-Skegness excursion, 22 May 1956. GEOFF KING

161. *Bottom right* In the days when locals still ran, the line looks positively prosperous, as 64301 leaves Thurnby station on 9 August 1950, with the 1400 Grantham-Belgrave Road. This train connected with the 'up' *Flying Scotsman* at Grantham! ALEC FORD

Opposite

162. *Top left* Looking back in the opposite direction to plate 161, 61142 is seen from the platform end, hauling another east-coast holiday special into Thurnby, August 1962. ALEC FORD

163. *Bottom left* Casually ambling from station to station, with its twin-coach set, 65018 presents a very attractive picture, leaving Thurnby with Belgrave Road-Grantham morning 'express', 3 July 1951. Connecting with the Edinburgh express at Grantham, this provided a faster Leicester-York service than the more direct route via the Midland! ALEC FORD

164. *Top right* Merrily polluting the atmosphere, J6 64248, with another twin-set, bowls along as the 1300 (SO) Belgrave Road-John O'Gaunt local, 3 December 1955. GEOFF KING

165. *Bottom right* The rural and rolling nature of the east Leicestershire countryside was the main reason for withdrawal of local services, and this terrain is apparent as 64213 leaves Ingarsby station with its two-coach train, 23 August 1952. ALEC FORD

Opposite

166. *Top left* Although only a small rural station, the GN obviously had hopes of greater things, with the facilities at Ingarsby-for-Houghton station being built to generous proportions and to attractive design, as seen in the early Fifties. ALEC FORD

167. *Bottom left* By 1956 the station at Ingarsby could do with a weeding, as 61283 heads a Whit Monday Belgrave Road-Mablethorpe excursion, 21 May 1956. GEOFF KING

168. *Top* An interloper onto the GN, MR 43107 looks set to do battle with the grasses, hauling the 1352 (SO) Mablethorpe-Belgrave Road and approaching Lowesby station, 27 June 1959. MIKE MITCHELL

169. *Bottom* Lowesby station is beginning to succumb to the ravages of time and neglect in this view of 61141 heading the 1318 (SO) Skegness-Belgrave Road, 25 August 1962. MIKE MITCHELL

170. *Top left* Marefield Junction signalbox, seen from the LRHS brakevan trip of 2 July 1960, was isolated and in the middle of nowhere, but was important in controlling the branch to Belgrave Road and the 'main line'. BARRY HILTON

171. *Centre* Another LRHS trip visited Tilton, after closure on 11 June 1963, and some of the party can be seen examining the largely extant station architecture. BARRY HILTON

172. *Bottom left* Another station visited on 11 June 1963 was John O'Gaunt, then still with sidings although closed to passengers. BARRY HILTON

Opposite

173. *Top right* MR 48736 breasts the bank near Marefield Junction with a southbound goods, May 1960. MIKE MITCHELL

174. *Bottom right* Another 8F passes what surely must have been one of the most unusual signal posts in the county! 48398 heads south away from Melton Mowbray North in the early Fifties. ALEC FORD

175. *Top* The more standard view of Melton Mowbray North station, 64269 drifts through the station with a 'down' freight, 4 July 1959, past station awnings that still look impressive despite being past their prime. BARRY HILTON

176. *Bottom* Heading away from the more northerly parts of the county, 61177 draws the 1318 (SO) Skegness-Belgrave Road out of Hose Tunnel at the foot of an impressive embankment, 21 July 1962. MIKE MITCHELL

177. *Top* On a very dull day, and with a right mixture of coaching stock, 43062 approaches Stathern Ironstone sidings, past another delightful GN somersault signal, with a Skegness-Belgrave Road train in the early Sixties. GEOFF KING

178. *Bottom* Evidencing the different nature of traffic in the northern reaches of the line, 63754 drags an iron-ore train away from the Eaton Quarries and takes the Scalford line at Wycombe Junction, 21 June 1960. GEOFF KING

179. *Top* With a packed train of enthusiasts behind, 'Standard' Class 4 75059 makes a rare visit to Waltham-on-the-Wold branch, as *The Leicestershire Woldsman* special, 19 June 1960.
GEOFF KING

180. *Bottom* Later in the day, the special reaches Scalford on the return journey, past a very unusual looking somersault signal.
GEOFF KING

4
Other Lines

Opposite

181. *Top left* One of my very first trips away from Leicester was a day trip to Rugby on a train just such as this. Stalwart of Leicester Midland (15C) shed and the Rugby service, 42331 heads the 1628 (FX) Rugby Midland-Leicester (London Road) at Wigston Central Junction, over the Wigston Magna-Glen Parva curve, 28 August 1961. GEOFF KING

182. *Bottom left* Cyclists on their way home from work have to wait at the crossing at Wigston South station for the 1745 Leicester-Rugby train to enter the staggered 'up' platform, behind 42062, 27 March 1961. MIKE MITCHELL

183. *Top* Prior to the 1955 Modernisation Plan, the LMSR wanted a diesel for branch line and light duty work. 10800 was designed and produced and is seen here on a Rugby-Leicester turn, approaching Wigston South, 9 November 1957. It was not totally successful and, after being tried on Birmingham-Norwich cross-country services, it was withdrawn in August 1959, later being sold to Brush Engineering (see Chapter 5). GEOFF KING

184. *Bottom* Unusual motive power for the branch, 40402, then Leicester (London Road) station pilot, has been seconded to replace a failed 2-6-4T, and is seen leaving Wigston South on the way to Rugby in the mid-Fifties. GEOFF KING

185. *Top left* Another view of 42331, this time leaving Countesthorpe with the 1633 Rugby-Leicester, 3 June 1961. MIKE MENSING

186. *Bottom left* In its latter days, DMUs were tried on the line in an attempt to reduce running costs and this view of a two-car unit entering Countesthorpe, on the way to Rugby, became a common sight. GEOFF KING

187. *Above* On the last day of all scheduled trains on the line, Saturday, 30 December 1961, 42331 – again! – was on duty to haul the *Leicester Railway Society Special* to Rugby, seen here pausing in the snow for guests to visit the station at Countesthorpe. HORACE GAMBLE

188. *Above* For some time after closure, the branch was used as a store for unwanted wagons, but by 30 May 1964 the tracks had been lifted and Nature begins to reclaim Countesthorpe station. ROGER THWAITES

Opposite

189. *Top right* The Nuneaton branch left the Midland main line at Wigston North Junction, where 45238 can be seen taking that branch line with a Leicester-Dudley excursion on Whit Tuesday, 1963. The tracks in the foreground are for the now-closed Rugby branch. GEOFF KING

190. *Bottom right* In 1986, after having had two decades of lost local stations, the county actually gained a new station, at South Wigston in May. 'Sprinter' 150114 enters the station on Wednesday, 12 October 1988, forming a Coventry-Nottingham train. HORACE GAMBLE

191. *Above* The 1610 Leicester-Nuneaton (Trent Valley) was often double-headed despite its short length, as shown here behind 45237 and 40087, approaching Wigston (Glen Parva) station, 22 August 1959. The lines to the right serve Wigston Central and South Junctions. MIKE MENSING

Opposite

192. *Top right* Unrebuilt 'Patriots' were never common to the Midland lines and certainly not on freight. 45533 *Lord Rathmore* passes through Wigston (Glen Parva) station on this dubious honour, bound for the more familiar West Coast route in the early 1960s. CHRIS BANKS' COLLECTION

193. *Bottom right* Unlike the Rugby branch, the Nuneaton line managed to retain its passenger service, which by the late 1980s had been entrusted to a mixture of DMUs. With one car painted in NSE livery, a Kettering-Birmingham mixed passenger/parcels train approaches Glen Parva Junction between the sites of Wigston Magna and Glen Parva stations, 19 October 1988.
HORACE GAMBLE

194. *Above* With the ex-GC main line overbridge in the background, 31200 heads the 1535 Norwich-Birmingham (New Street), ½ mile east of Narborough, on Bank Holiday Monday, 26 August 1974. MIKE MENSING

Opposite

195. *Top right* Narborough station still has much of the feel of steam days, with buildings largely intact, as 47194 heads the 1015 Birmingham (NS)-Norwich into the platform, 14 January 1984. CHRIS MILNER

196. *Bottom right* By the end of the Eighties, loco-hauled passenger trains were becoming something of a rarity, with this service handed over to 'Sprinters'. The 1M68 1414 Yarmouth-Birmingham (NS) passes Croft behind 31290 and 31233, double power needed for the ten coaches, Saturday, 14 August 1982. HORACE GAMBLE

197. *Top left* Double-headed 37s on passenger are also a rarity. At the head of F&W Railtours' *Skeggy Buckateer*, originating in Plymouth, 37233 and 37186 look in fine fettle passing Burbage Common, en route for Skegness, 1 July 1984. CHRIS MILNER

198. *Bottom left* Also unusual is a 58 on passenger. On another special over the Nuneaton branch, 58014 passes Hinckley, having joined the train at Birmingham en route from Cardiff-Cleethorpes, 15 July 1984. CHRIS MILNER

199. *Top* The branch to Coalville and Burton-on-Trent lost its passenger service in September 1964, but such is the growing problem with car saturation of the roads in and around Leicester that talk at the close of the Eighties was for re-opening of passenger services and stations on the route. In happier days, 75059 approaches Saffron Lane crossing, with the 0822 Leicester-Burton parcels, which included one passenger coach, Wednesday, 16 August 1961. HORACE GAMBLE

200. *Bottom* Just a little further and the line crossed the GC main line. About to reach this spot and accelerating hard, 42182 heads the 1220 Leicester-Burton local, 12 April 1958. BARRY HILTON

201. *Top left* Kirby Muxloe was truly a delightful station with its mixture of fine architecture and greenery, as can be seen from this view of 5 September 1964.
BARRY HILTON

202. *Bottom left* Although without passengers for over two decades, the line is heavily used by freight, although now single track. The guard of 56065 seems to be totally relaxed about it all, reading his paper as the Cliffe Hill-Hayes & Harlington Tarmac Roadstone train approaches the site of Kirby Muxloe station, Friday, 4 November 1988. HORACE GAMBLE

Opposite

203. *Top right* It is hardly surprising that the fireman of 48690 looks unhurried, in view of the length of the train as they amble eastwards, just east of Bagworth & Ellistown station, 11 May 1963.
MIKE MENSING

204. *Bottom right* In the early days of DMUs, warnings on the front were either in the form of 'whiskers', or a small yellow panel, as shown on a Craven set approaching Bagworth & Ellistown station on the 1655 Leicester-Burton local, 11 May 1963. MIKE MENSING

207. *Above* At Coalville shed, 17 October 1965, D5255 and D7537 have an opportunity to compare notes as they stand face to face between duties. JOHN COOPER-SMITH

Overleaf

208. *Top left* With the possible reopening of the stations along the route, as a partial answer to the car, Moira station could once again echo to the sound of railway customers. On 24 April 1974, however, this seems a very remote possibility, despite the buildings still being extant. MIKE MENSING

209. *Bottom left* Part of the problem and part of the salvation for the line. The MGR coal trains earn big money for the line, but the extraction of the coal has dramatic effects on the line itself, as can be seen by the 'switchback' track beneath 56081, heading west with a trip to Coalfields Farm, 1 July 1983. COLIN MARSDEN

210. *Top right* Only towards the Eighties have 'Choppers' been downgraded to more secondary duties. 20037 and 20169 haul a train of power station slack westwards at Moira West Junction, 24 April 1974. MIKE MENSING

211. *Bottom right* Having completed one tour of duty, 20199 and 20076 take the spur to the south at Moira West Junction, 24 April 1974. Interestingly, 20199 is without a cab-side number. MIKE MENSING

Opposite

205. *Top left* Although hated by steam enthusiasts, DMUs have given valuable sterling service over the years and there is a certain nostalgic charm in this 2-car set, seen moving away from the entrance to the Shackerstone branch as the 1548 Leicester-Burton, south-east of Coalville, 11 May 1963. MIKE MENSING

206. *Bottom left* For many years, Class 20s ('Choppers') have been ever reliable and popular. 20188 and 20082 take a train of HAA wagons away from NCB Snibston at the Exchange Sidings, Coalville, Thursday, 12 May 1983. HORACE GAMBLE

214. *Above* A picture full of interest. Barely a year after this view, the Birmingham-East Anglia trains were handed over to Sprinter DMUs; on 4 June 1987, though, loco-hauled was still the order of the day, as 31403, forming the 1220 Birmingham (NS)-Ipswich service, slows for the Melton Mowbray stop, passing the rather precarious looking signalbox. BRIAN MORRISON

Opposite

212. Looking west from Melton Junction, so much has disappeared that once seemed so common and permanent. The unfitted freight, with its ubiquitous guard's van; the gangers so casual in normal working clothes, without the high visibility vests; semaphores, track-side allotments and even the Class of engines. And the line to the right, once reaching Nottingham, now only used to Old Dalby and the test track. D7500 and D5297 head towards Melton Mowbray station, destined eventually for Corby, 11 May 1972. JOHN COOPER-SMITH

213. Looking east from the same vantage point in the early days of dieselisation of freights, when brake-tenders were necessary to supplement the loco's inadequate braking system, D1866 leaves Melton Mowbray on a Corby-Toton train of iron-ore empties, August 1966. JOHN COOPER-SMITH

215. *Above* Looking down on the station, past that same
signalbox, 20032 and 20188 pass through on a 'down' train of
empty hoppers, 4 June 1987. BRIAN MORRISON

Opposite

216. *Top right* The bitterly cold conditions can almost be felt
from this shot of 45062 on an 'up' coal train, seen passing
through Melton Mowbray station on Thursday, 9 January 1986.
HORACE GAMBLE

217. *Bottom right* On a heavy train of ballast, originating at
Mountsorrel, 47323 clears Melton Mowbray station, heading
east, 4 June 1987. BRIAN MORRISON

218. *Above* Much trade is given to BR by Petfoods at Melton Mowbray and some of their wagons can be seen in the background, as 31465 heads a train of empty hoppers bound for Mountsorrel and a refill, on the approach to Melton station, 4 June 1987. BRIAN MORRISON

219. *Above* The Lackenby-Corby steel coil train was one of the most celebrated freights of the Eighties, with photographers flocking to capture its various permutations of Class 37/5 locos. On 4 June 1987, 37502 *British Steel Teeside* leads sister 37501 *Teeside Steelmaster* on the curved approach to Melton Mowbray station. BRIAN MORRISON

220. *Top left* The staged nuclear flask crash of 17 July 1984 was widely publicised and covered by the media, and was a remarkable piece of public relations by the CEGB. After the smash, 46009 is barely recognisable at the Old Dalby site.
COLIN MARSDEN

221. *Bottom left* After the 'show' was over, invited celebrities were returned to St Pancras behind 45123 *The Lancashire Fusilier*, which waits at Grimston Tunnel, Old Dalby, for the parties to board.
COLIN MARSDEN

222. *Top right* The Charnwood Forest Railway line from Coalville-Loughborough was worked by the LNWR from the outset, as the original company was adjudged bankrupt. Opened in 1883, passenger services were withdrawn in 1931 and freight progressively withdrawn between 1955 and 1963. I knew the line briefly from 1957-61, but never saw Loughborough (Derby Road) station like this, seen in 1951, the year of cessation of excursion traffic. ALEC FORD

223. *Bottom right* On the same day in 1951, MR Class 4F 44091 shunts the goods yard at Loughborough. ALEC FORD

Opposite

224. *Top left* The three-road shed at
Loughborough still has track into one
door, but this has obviously not been used
for many a year, although the building has
been put to good use. 1951. ALEC FORD

225. *Bottom left* Still with 'LMS' on the
tender, despite being three years into
Nationalisation, 44091 shunts its heavy
load by the shed, with track seemingly
going in all directions! ALEC FORD

226. *Top right* The real work is just
beginning, as 44091 brings the morning
goods past the engine shed. ALEC FORD

227. *Bottom right* The LRS *21st Anniversary
Special* gets around and now lets its guests
step out and inspect Shepshed station,
whilst 41321 waits to continue. 27 May
1961. BARRY HILTON

228. *Top* What a modeller's delight is Whitwick station, even down to the doors used as window boarding (right). Although not seeing regular passengers for twenty years, the station and fittings appear in remarkably good condition, perhaps because, for a time, it was used as an ironmonger's shop! 1951. ALEC FORD

229. *Bottom* Maybe a little gaunt, Coalville East station, nevertheless, looks very attractive alongside yet more crossing on the level in 1951. ALEC FORD

5
Hatch and Despatch

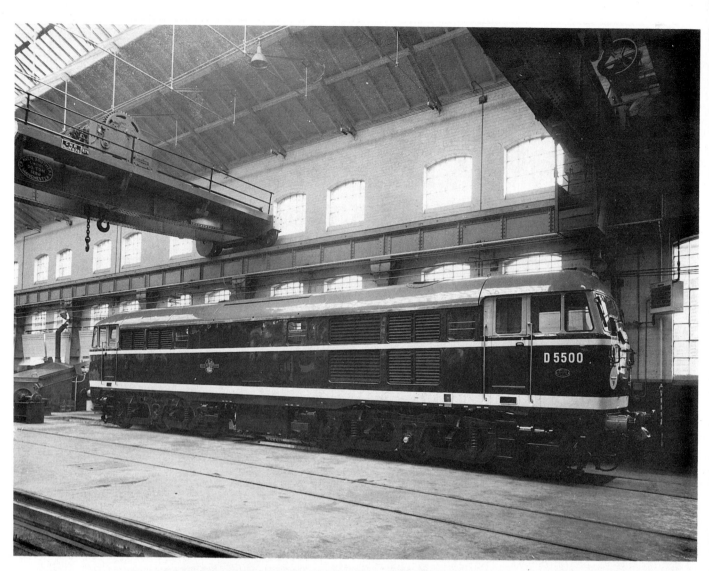

232. *Above* A hive of activity in the days when heavy engineering was commonplace. Two D58xxs are well on their way to completion, alongside *Falcon*, in the workshop, 4 July 1961. BEM

Overleaf

233. *Top left* Eight months after the previous view and *Falcon*, now allocated D0280 by BR, stands in the works compound at Brush (with the GC main line in the background) in its original coat of lime green and chestnut brown. Having been originally released to BR in September 1961 with a transfer nameplate, it had returned to Brush in March 1962 for inspection, when it was fitted with cast alloy nameplates. 26 March 1962. BEM

234. *Bottom left* *Falcon* having been accepted by the British Transport Commission as the Type 4 it wanted from the various prototypes put forward, Brush began the production run, with slight modifications. What was to become Class 47 began with D1500 seen here in preliminary coat and hastily constructed number plate. Loughborough, September 1962. BEM

235. *Top right* By 20 September 1962, D1500 has received its final livery and number transfer, and stands in Brush's back lot with D5858, also newly completed. BEM

236. *Bottom right* Originally a run of twenty, the Type 2s finally numbered 263 examples, with the last one, D5862, leaving the works, as seen here, 25 October 1962. BEM

Opposite

230. *Top left* Although Brush Engineering have been building locomotives, initially steam, since the late nineteenth century, it is only since the days of the Type 2 diesels for BR (later Class 31), that the Company has had much of a public profile and awareness. D5500 was the prototype and is seen here in original condition, as delivered to British Railways in September 1957, part of an order for twenty locos. BEM

231. *Bottom left* Another view of D5500 (centre) under construction, together with sisters D5501 (left) and D5505 (right – frame only), in Brush workshops, Loughborough in 1957. BEM

Opposite

237. *Top left* As with the Type 2s, the Type 4s were for an original run of twenty, although this was very quickly expanded to fifty. The latter part of the first twenty are in various stages of construction in the super-structure shop, 15 December 1962. BEM

238. *Bottom left* As with any new design, extensive tests were carried out with the Type 4s. In pouring rain, returning 'home', D1504 passes through Loughborough station with a dynamometer car and ten-coach train in May 1963. BEM

239. *Above* Originally built 1948-50, but to a design from the LMS, 10800 did not last too long, having moved between Regions on trials and finally settling on the Midland Region. Having worked such services as Birmingham-Norwich, Leicester-Rugby and inter-regional freights, it was withdrawn in August 1959. Brush bought it in the early Sixties for experimentation and is seen under test, 3 June 1963. BEM

240. *Bottom right* Late in 1964 it was given a major body rebuild and was repainted into a 'mid' green livery, shown here inside Brush Works. Having spent time at Rugby Testing Station, and then work on the GC, it finally gave up in 1968. BEM

241. *Above* Bearing Works plate number 444, D1682 stands
outside the Brush Falcon Works in Loughborough, still in two-
tone green, the first of the contract for the Western Region.
15 October 1963. BEM

242. *Above* With the odd loco bound for Rhodesian Railways in
between rows of Type 4s near completion, 1 July 1964. BEM

Overleaf

243. *Top left* In November 1963, having completed its British
Railways testing, D0280 *Falcon* returned to Brush. It reappeared
in January 1965, but now painted in Brunswick green, with small
yellow warning panels, shown here on the 'up' freight line at
Loughborough station, 27 January 1965. BEM

244. *Bottom left* In 1965, the Brush-powered 'Peaks', later Class
46, were called to Brush for attention. On 23 September 1965,
eight of their number receive the remedial work, including
D168, D182 and D176. More Type 4s near completion to the
rear of the shop. BEM

245. *Top right* One of the very first Type 4s to be painted in the
corporate blue polyurethane, D1958 stands in the bright
sunshine of 4 January 1967, outside Brush Works. BEM

246. *Bottom right* Numbers 99 and 100 of the current batch of
Type 4s stand in company with the latest prototype *Kestrel*, the
latter showing definite advances in design. Brush, Loughborough,
23 January 1967. BEM

249. *Above* Not having built locomotives in any number for BR for some years, 1989 saw the agreement to build the new freight engines needed for the 1990s and beyond – the Class 60. Shrouded in photographic secrecy within Brush's workshop, 60001 has not long arrived from Procor for the power unit etc, to be fitted. 3 March 1989.

Opposite

247. *Top left* As with the Type 4s, *Kestrel*, allocated HS4000 (derived from the initials of Hawker Siddeley – who now owned Brush – and the engines' 4000hp power output), spent many hours on BR tracks on test. An undoubted success, despite slight problems with axle loading, it was an impressive and very powerful locomotive, but its potential was never fully realised in this country, as it was sold to Russia in 1971! In its BR days, in the distinctive brown and yellow livery, it passes through Loughborough on test, under the GC metals, 5 September 1968. BEM

248. *Bottom left* Many years later, Brush designed yet another winning locomotive, this time electric, 89001, later to be named *Avocet*, to celebrate the centenary of RSPB and to keep up the birds' names tradition of Brush prototypes. It spent time on test from Crewe before going to the ECML, and is seen leaving Loughborough by road, bound for Crewe, in 1988. NEVILLE MAYS

250. *Above* In the 1980s, Vic Berry's scrapyard on the site of the old goodsyard, adjacent to the ex-GC main line, became a Mecca for enthusiasts. To help move the stock around the yard, Berry bought ex-BR 03 shunter 03069 and this is seen resting from duties on Sunday, 30 September 1984.

Opposite

251. *Top right* Perhaps the most unusual and 'glamorous' stock for Leicestershire was the Class 82 and 83 electrics, cut up in 1984. Outwardly in excellent shape, 83002, 83010, 83007 and 83001 (right to left), stand under an ominous sky, awaiting their painful fate, on 4 November 1984.

252. *Bottom right* Such was the speed at which Vic Berry was accepting coaching stock for cutting in 1985, that it had to be piled up, whilst other items were dealt with. 303059 has lost its bogies and will soon lose everything else! 18 August 1985.

253. *Top left* Class 45s began to disappear at more rapid rates as the Eighties wore on, and an unidentified member has had the rough treatment, dumped amongst Class 25 cabs, 28 December 1986.

254. *Bottom left* Another 45, 45003, seems to raise its head in defiance, despite being gutted, 1 March 1987.

Opposite

Two views of 25060 on April 1987.

255. *Top right* Having been robbed of bogies, one end nosedives into the ground; whilst . . .

256. *Bottom right* Apart from the missing buffers, the loco looks almost normal from the other end.

257. *Above* With sad expressions, the cabs of 27009, 27032 and 26003 (left to right) seem to be in conversation, 5 April 1987.

258. *Above* The infamous pile. In 1987, the influx of locos even outstripped the speed of coaches and certainly the speed of cutters. To store them, Vic piled them high and caused a real landmark in the county, with photographers flocking from near and far to capture the scene. As well as 27022 (left), there are 43 on the pile(!), including (extreme right; top to bottom) 25285, 25052 and 25089, 26 September 1987.

259. *Above* Seen among the twisted metal rubbish that always seemed to litter the site, 45065 hardly looks as though it is a candidate for the scrapheap, 7 August 1988.

Opposite

260. *Top right* In October 1988, two Class 31s ran away, unattended, at Cricklewood in north London, fell down an embankment and came to rest with 31202 underneath its sister. Two days after the accident, on 30 October 1988, some of the damage can be assessed from this view, after the engine had arrived at Leicester.

261. *Bottom right* The end that fared worst, with the cab well and truly damaged beyond repair.

262. *Top left* During 1988, the loco pile changed, shrank and was then supplemented by 45s and 20s. Top dogs on 30 October 1988 were 27023 and 25095; with 27025 and 27053 clearly visible on the ends of their rows.

263. *Bottom left* An unidentified 45, bereft of rear end, squats in the yard, with crash victim 31202 in the background, 30 October 1988.

264. *Top right* As well as coaches and locos, Vic Berry also deals with DMUs and EMUs. Ex-4 REP Class 430 unit 3008 (MS coach 62155 leading), stands outside the working yard, awaiting its call, 30 October 1988.

265. *Bottom right* Two of the developments of the yard in 1988 was the growth of work de-asbestosing stock for both BR and the preservation movement, and the start of contracts to paint locos, coaches and multiple units for BR. The very first of the latter, 31275, from the Crewe nuclear flask fleet and adorned with coal sector markings, stands on display by Upperton Road bridge. 9 October 1988.

266. *Above* Looking like some bug-eyed monster, 31130 is masked and in yellow undercoat in one of the paint shops put up on site, 30 October 1988.